Nicholas Breakspear (Adrian IV) Englishman and Pope

force the clergy to support themselves on the freewill offerings of the people He could conceive of no other use for property than that it should be held by the sovereign for the common good. A great Christian commonwealth with laws modelled on the best of the ancient philosophy; Rome the centre of the world in all her old time grandeur , everyone working for the good of all, and no one for the transitory purposes of his own immediate gain. "A beautiful Utopia indeed ' " one is almost tempted to exclaim, but one which, like all other theories based on an equality which does not exist, will, as long as human nature shall endure, be realized in the imagination only If, at the close of the nineteenth century, amid all the potent forces of our boasted civilization, we regard the Socialist and the Liberator as dreamers, what name can we apply to the man who attempted to promulgate such doctrines among the untutored intellects and savage natures of the early mediæval times ? And it is only just to point out that, like all dreamers, Arnold was one-sided in his judgment , his enthusiasm only enabled him to see the abuse of riches in the Church, and failed to show him that she must, if she was to live, have the means necessary to carry out her mission, to keep up her dignity, to relieve her poorer members, and to maintain the worship of God , not to mention the training of her sons and the mission work of bringing fresh sheep to the fold.

We must now revert to the Council of Sens, and trace Arnold's subsequent career. Bernard, in ordering the condemnation of Abelard, decreed also that Arnold should be incarcerated in a convent, but he managed to evade the authorities and fled to Zurich, then, owing to its freedom and its proximity to the republics of Lombardy, as well as to its trade with both Germany and Italy, the most flourishing town in Switzerland, and from that place, where he was enthusiastically received, he preached and spread his new doctrine. The tide of public opinion was in his favour, and everywhere events were quickening to help on his career of reform

In the city of Brescia a conflict between bishop, as representing the imperial interests, and people had resulted in the defeat of the former Innocent II, a somewhat weak man, hesitated, and at length, perhaps hoping to quiet things by concessions, or because he regarded the Emperor as a more serious foe than Arnold, leant towards the populace This strengthened the hands of Arnold enormously, and his preaching became more and more socialistic Whether his ideas were properly understood by the people is doubtful, but matters little; they at least comprehended that the immediate result of his teaching would be to take the wealth from the clerical party and to place it in their own hands Arnold was proclaimed a liberator · his name was honoured, and his praises were in everyone's mouth The man who preaches a doctrine of spoliation, which, however disinterested or noble in conception, tends to weaken the distinction between " meum " and ' tuum, is always assured of a considerable following

In Rome itself the spirit of independence was growing

rapidly   Tivoli, Palestrina, Tusculum, and Albano had all
tried to throw off the Roman yoke and secure their independence, and in 1143 the Romans themselves, on
Innocent II concluding a treaty with the first-named
city against their wishes, burst out into open rebellion,
defied the Church's authority, and set up a senate which
declared the papal government at an end and the ancient
republic restored   Innocent tried hard to make head
against this movement, invoked a synod at the Lateran,
and made a protest ; but he had neither the spirit nor the
power to check the insubordination of the republicans, who
emboldened to further effort saw in their imagination Rome
restored to her former high place among the nations—
Rome the secular no less than the spiritual head of the
world   In the intoxication of their ambition they called on
the Emperor Conrad to return and take his place as their
king   Conrad, either doubting the fickle nature of a mob,
or because he feared the papal authority, refused, and
though all preparations were made for his coming, did not
appear, and perhaps lost thereby the chance of altering
the history of Rome. The same year saw the death of
Innocent, broken-hearted and full of grief   Celestine II,
who succeeded, had been himself a pupil of Abelard, and
moreover had, as Cardinal of Castello, befriended Arnold,
who took advantage of this to appear in Rome. Celestine
died only six months after his accession, and was succeeded
by Lucius II. a Bolognese by birth.   The republic,
strengthened by the peace of the short pontificate of his

predecessor, was more bold than ever, and announced to
the Pope their intention to acknowledge his spiritual
authority and nothing beyond. Lucius was a man of firm
character, but found it impossible to stem the rising tide,
which eventually assailed even his spiritual powers by
electing a brother of the Anti-pope Analectus to be
" Patrician," and to usurp the power of the papal prefect
The populace were delighted at this encroachment on the
power of the Church, and in the riots which ensued destroyed
many of the buildings in Rome, including some of the
palaces of the cardinals   Finally, in the year 1145, Lucius
II, going in person at the head of the pontifical troops to
expostulate with the rioters, in one of these outbreaks
was struck by a stone and killed

It was at this moment that Bernard of Clairvaulx
thought it necessary to step into the breach, and, as we have
seen, also thought that in electing Eugenius III, the Cistercian abbot, he had a tool ready made to his hands

I have already dwelt on the character of Eugenius;
he dealt with affairs as he found them with some firmness.
The Roman mob burst in upon his election, and angrily
demanded him to recognize the authority of the senate.
He made no answer, but left the city and the election was
completed at the Convent of Forsa   He then retired to
Viterbo, and from there commenced to launch anathemas
at his persecutors.   At length a reconciliation was effected,
the Pope agreeing to recognize the senate on condition
that those only whom he approved should be elected, and

that the patrician should give way to the papal legate
He triumphantly entered the Eternal City, and celebrated
Christmas, 1145   But the peace was short-lived, and fresh
riots taking place, he was compelled to flee from Rome

It may now be asked why Bernard did not come himself, and with his strong personality redress the evil state
into which the government had fallen   I think the answer
to this is to be found in the second crusade, to which I
have already alluded   He hoped by this to re-establish
the weakened power of the Church, and to a very considerable extent he succeeded.

Bernard had a very low opinion of the Romans.   He
says·[1] "What is so well known to the world as their
licence and pride . . . ."   "They are ever given to sedi-
tion." "They strive after the appearance of being feared by
all, while in fact they fear everybody."   And again, "They
cannot endure submission, but yet know not how to rule"
No doubt he expected the second crusade to right the wrong
at home as well as abroad   We know how disastrously it
failed in the Holy Land; but it produced consequences of
some moment.   The Pope, being brought into close con-
tact with the most powerful sovereigns of Europe, had
taken advantage of the opportunity to make alliances and
to strengthen his authority.   The Romans, who had at
first laughed at the papal displeasure, were gradually
beginning to regret their hasty action, when they saw

[1] "De Consideratione," lib iv , cap 2

N

that it led to the glories of Rome as the centre of the religious world being transferred to other places and to other countries, and many of those who had been foremost in the revolution began to have doubts as to whether they had not paid too great a price for civil liberty Eugenius, whose firm nature was combined with generosity and mildness, was until his death in 1153 becoming more and more popular Bernard of Clairvaulx and his Cistercian namesake died in the same year, the former never recovering from the shock of the failure of his efforts to free the Holy Land, he leaves behind him the foremost name in the history of the Church of the twelfth century.

Anastasius IV, as we have seen, enjoyed a reign free from internal troubles, and we may now look round on the aspect of affairs which the new Pope had to face

Arnold of Brescia had found his power much undermined during the reign of Eugenius but Rome was still governed by the senate, and as then mouthpiece Arnold had, on the death of the Emperor Conrad, invited his successor, Frederic Barbarossa, nephew of Conrad, to come and receive the imperial crown from the senate The great Emperor refused, owing to the insolent terms in which the letter was worded, whereupon the republic determined by the advice of Arnold to choose an emperor for themselves.

No additional incentive was required to induce Frederic to cross the Alps and reassert the power of the emperor over Italy Frederic Barbarossa is another of the brilliant cluster of commanding men who lived at this period He

was a prince of the most unbounded ambition, proud,
assertive, and powerful, unquestionably the most striking
figure among those who have ever worn the iron crown.
His strong will was well suited to overcome every obstacle,
and now his intention was to assert his absolute supremacy
in Italy as in Germany, and, above all, to be crowned in
Rome by the Pope.

Just before Adrian's election by the cardinals, namely,
in November, 1154, Barbarossa crossed the Alps at the
head of a large and imposing army, accompanied by all the
rough knighthood of his Teutonic subjects, and on the
plains of Roncaglia summoned all the feudatories of the
Empire to do homage City after city, petty republics,
domains and territories passed one by one into his hands.
What would he do when he arrived before Rome ?

No wonder, then, that on the death of the peaceful old
Pope Anastasius IV. the cardinals looked round for a
strong man to meet the critical state of affairs in and
outside of Rome. Nicholas Breakspear was the man of
all others for the position. They wanted a statesman and
diplomatist, as well as a ruler of firmness and unquestioned
integrity to steer the Holy Church and her fortunes through
this crisis in her history; and such a man was he whom
they had chosen. Of quite a different stamp from the
venerable father who had just passed away; a man of
singular courage, who could take occasion by the horns,
who had always boldly kept to a high idea of duty, and
who had just returned from a most successful mission to

the barbaric North, he was not a man likely to truckle
to a Roman mob, or even to lower his head before the
mighty Barbarossa   In the next chapter we shall see how
Adrian IV. rose to his position, and how he dealt with
those problems in the condition of Rome, the growth of
which I have endeavoured to describe

CHAPTER VI.

1154 TO 1155.

Adrian's Difficulties—Cardinal Boso—Arnold of Brescia in Rome—
The Interdict—Adrian's Entry into Rome—Easter, 1155—Advance of
Frederic Barbarossa—Negotiations between Pope and Emperor—Capture
and Death of Arnold of Brescia—Roman Deputation to Frederic—Adrian
proceeds to meet the Emperor at Sutri.

THE first difficulty Adrian IV. had to meet on his succession was that of the peremptory demand of the senate, prompted by Arnold of Brescia, that the Pope should recognize the temporal authority of the republic. Thus the problem was at once presented to him, was he to rule, or were the people? As might be expected from what we know of Breakspear's previous action, he rose to the occasion; stern and unyielding, he hurled back at the deputation his defiance of their pretensions, and announcing that no compromise was possible, and that he and he only would lead the Roman people and be their head, he dismissed them haughtily from his presence. The idea of bargaining with those whom he regarded merely as disaffected subjects never entered his mind.

Arnold of Brescia on this returned to Rome, and once

more began to inflame the popular mind with his revolu-
tionary doctrines, and to preach resistance against the
Pope's decree.   Adrian had conceived the loftiest notions
of his power, and like Bernard was determined that the
Church should be supreme.   After his meeting with the
envoys of the senate, he retired to Anagni and prepared
for war.   Here we cannot do better than read the description
of his triumph over the followers of Arnold which has come
down to us from the pen of his secretary, Cardinal Boso,
an actual eye-witness of the scenes which he records   As
I have said before, this Boso was a nephew of Adrian,
and had been his secretary for some time   Perhaps some
details of his life may be of interest, and fortunately in
Ciaconius[1] there is a very good account, which, in a list of
Adrian's first creation of cardinals, runs as follows   " Boso
(English), a nephew of Adrian IV, Pope, and, according
to Ughell and John Pits, ' de scriptoribus ecclesiasticis
Angliæ,' his clerk   He was formerly a Benedictine monk
at S. Albans   Raised by Adrian IV to be cardinal deacon
of S Côme et S Damien, and a chancellor of the church

     " Further created cardinal presbyter with the title of San
Pudenziana by Alexander III[2]   He was held in warm esteem
by the first-named Pope, who, when he had reason to suspect
the Emperor and Roman people of playing him false,
entrusted to him the custody of his stronghold in S Peter's

---

[1] Prima creatio cardinalium Hadriani Quarti Papæ   Anno 1155
Ciaconius, tom 1, p 1064
[2] Adrian IV.'s successor, 1158

"After Adrian's death he was a principal agent in securing the election of Alexander III., whose claims against the Anti-pope Octavian he warmly advocated. On Octavian's pseudo-election, he took under his protection all those cardinals who refused to recognize the schismatist, and gave them shelter from the popular anger in the castle of S Angelo, which—as we have already said—had been entrusted to him by Adrian.

"Here he kept them until the fury of the mob had subsided, when he released them, upon which they promptly declared Alexander III. to have been duly elected Pope by them. He attended Alexander III. constantly, especially at Venice, and directed all his efforts towards the attainment of peace Pope Innocent III mentions in the first volume of his register that Boso was sent as a legate to Portugal, while Alexander IV also mentions that he performed a legation in Alexander III.'s pontificate He died towards the end of Alexander III.'s reign, or, if we accept John Pit's version, in the time of Lucius III., that is to say, about 1181.

"He was buried at Rome. As a clerk of the Church he wrote a diploma which Eugenius III. gave to the canons of S. Peter; afterwards, in his capacity of cardinal, he subscribed many papal letters, both of Adrian IV and Alexander III. He was a pious man and a learned, and contemporary English writers may well rank him among the foremost ecclesiastics of his time."

I have mentioned before that Adrian probably met

him on his way through England to Norway he was,
in all probability, sent by him to Rome with letters to
Eugenius III , and was one of those who greeted the
" Apostle of the North " on his return

The account of Boso runs as follows [1] "About this time
the famous heretic, Arnold of Brescia, boldly entered the
city, and began to sow the poisonous seeds of his heresy
among the ignorant, whose minds he sought to seduce from
the true way of life   This man had caused incessant trouble
to Eugenius and Anastasius, both of whom had tried hard
to expel him , but so cunningly had he ingratiated himself
with the citizens, and more particularly with the senators—
who at this time were elected by popular vote—that all
efforts to dislodge him were vain : and now, in the face of
Adrian's strict prohibition, he insolently tarried in the city "
—Adrian had issued a peremptory command for him to leave
—"laying his plots and openly declaring his hostility to the
Pope   But the culminating point was reached when the
venerable Cardinal Guido, Presbyter of S Potentienne, was
openly attacked on the Via Sacra while on his way to the
papal presence, and dangerously wounded by some impious
follower of Arnold. The Pope immediately laid Rome under
an interdict, and forbade the observance of any holy office
until the Wednesday of Holy Week.   Then were the
senators impelled by the voice of clergy and laity alike
to prostrate themselves before his Holiness, who made

[1] Hadriani IV , Vita, apud Card Boso, ed. Migne

them swear a solemn oath that they would drive forth the heretic of whom we have been speaking, together with all his followers, and chase them from the confines of Rome, unless they, the heretics, undertook to return immediately in obedience to the jurisdiction of the Holy Father This was done The heretics were cast forth, and the ban of interdiction removed from the city.   Immediately a great joy came upon the people, who fell to praising the Lord and blessing Him with one voice And on the following day, the anniversary of our Lord's supper, while on all sides men flocked to receive the annual absolution of their sins as they were wont, the venerable Pontiff, attended by an immense suite of bishops, cardinals, and nobles, and followed by thousands of the laity, came forth in state from the Leonine city, in which he had held his court ever since the day of his ordination, and took up his abode amid expressions of universal joy in the Lateran of his predecessors.   Here he remained six days— Good Friday, Saturday, Easter Day, and Monday, Tuesday, and Wednesday in Easter week—celebrating the holy rites of the Church, and eating the passover with his clergy in the Lateran Palace, according to the time-honoured custom of the Church.   And when at last the period of glad festivity had drawn to a close, each one returned home with gladness in his heart."

Adrian had shown his power indeed ! Let us recapitulate The haughty decree for Arnold to leave the city had produced the usual riots, but without frightening the man who sat in the papal chair. He is sterner than ever, and as

o

unyielding   Then came the assault on old Cardinal Guido
at the hands of the mob, precipitating the crisis, and causing
the storm to break   A cardinal is dead, but remember,
some years before the Roman rioters had slain the Pope
himself   And now Adrian brings up all the forces of the
Church—"Ready to smite once and smite no more."   The
rising feeling against the Church must be crushed, the whole
might of the spiritual authority must be used, the force em-
ployed so colossal as to pulverize the body of discontent
arising from heretical teaching and prevent it from ever
again being revived; and so he came to use the last great
weapon in his power, the interdict, never used in Rome
before   Adrian was not a man to be bound by precedents;
he laid down his own course, and kept to it; consulted no
man, bent to no ancient custom which would prevent his
free exercise of power

No calamity which could befall a city in those times
—and they were days when calamity had full meaning, days
of the storm and sack, of the plague and the famine—could
be more dreaded than that of an interdict.

Religious fervour might be failing; but the awe which
was inspired by the searching spiritual power of the Church
was as firmly rooted as ever it was in the minds of the
people, and an interdict brought all the terrors of the loss of
heavenly future, of prolongation of years in purgatory, and
the absence of the comforting rites of the Church.   Adrian
IV. chose his time well by commencing on Palm Sunday,
for all Europe flocked to Rome as a devout pilgrimage at

Easter time, and he thus struck a blow at the trade brought by them to the city—smote their earthly as well as their spiritual interests A Roman Catholic writer[1] has well described the condition of the city under the interdict, a description which I am tempted to repeat. He tells us that it commenced at midnight by the funereal and muffled tolling of the church bells; whereupon the entire clergy might presently be seen issuing forth, in silent procession, by torchlight, to put up a last prayer of deprecation before the altars for the guilty community Then the consecrated bread, that remained over, was burnt; the crucifixes and other sacred images were veiled up , the relics of the saints carried down into the crypts. Every memento of holy cheerfulness and peace was withdrawn from view. Lastly, a papal legate ascended the steps of the high altar arrayed in penitential vestments, and formally proclaimed the interdict From that moment divine service ceased in all the churches; their doors were locked up; and only in the bare porch might the priest, dressed in mourning, exhort his flock to repentance. Rites, in their nature joyful, which could not be dispensed with, were invested with sorrowful attributes; so that baptism could only be administered in secret, and marriage celebrated before a tomb instead of an altar The administration of confession and communion was forbidden. To the dying man alone might the viaticum, which the priest had first consecrated in the gloom and solitude of the morning dawn, be given; but extreme unction and burial

[1] R. Raby, 1849.

in holy ground were denied him Moreover, the interdict seriously affected the worldly as well as the religious cares of society Such, then, was the state to which Adrian boldly reduced the proud city of Rome At first the interdict was received with an assumption of bravado, which, however, as the gloomy days passed on, soon subsided into a deep feeling of terror and horror Men had time to reflect on the error of their ways Easter always heralded joy and forgiveness of sins · but this year it seemed as if the weight of fresh sins and their accompanying penalties were being added to the whole community, and as Holy Week drew near, and the people realized the awful idea that there would be no services in the churches, the mob veered round and completely surrendered all they had demanded, and more As Boso has told us, they greeted the triumphal entry of the Pope with joy and enthusiasm The heretic at last had met his match, and the world learnt something of the character of the man who was guiding the destinies of the Holy Church Firmness and prompt decision had conquered, as so long as the earth shall endure they always will, the changeable passions of a mob.

Adrian's terms before he would remove the interdict were absolute and exacting, and he gained all that he demanded Meeting the envoys of the populace-driven senate at Viterbo, he declined to listen to anything but a complete abrogation of the republic, the banishment of Arnold and his lieutenants, and the return of the citizens to absolute submission to the Pope The Church had conquered in the most complete manner

Arnold fled to the country, a disappointed and beaten man, and at Otricoli was taken prisoner by the Cardinal Gerhard of S Nicolas, but was rescued by one of the viscounts of the Campagna, who had obtained some estates by a grant from the republic properly belonging to the Pope, and under his protection, combined with that of other wild noblemen of that part of the Campagna, continued in a fitful way to try to stir up dissension in Rome Adrian was now approaching the central crisis of his life, ever since the autumn of 1154 had been heard the news of the slow but sure advance of the mighty Emperor Barbarossa through the rich plains of Lombardy A few short weeks after the triumph of Easter at Rome he had received the iron crown in the church of S Michael at Pavia;[1] some resistance had been made, but it was useless against the inflexible will of the advancing potentate. Lombardy was at his feet: Tortona the last city to fall after a brave and gallant resistance, and at length the Germanic hordes entered the northern marches of the Campagna Adrian viewed this advance with apprehension, and took all the measures he could, sending troops to fortify Viterbo, Orvieto, and Civita Castellana, but he knew that resistance would easily be overcome if the Emperor was really hostile, and he determined to act in accordance with the principles he had so recently declared with such effect; he put the spiritual side of his position foremost, and in this decision

[1] Easter Day in 1155 was March 27th. Frederic received the iron crown at Pavia on April 10th in that year.

showed not mere clever diplomacy, but the true spirit of statesmanship He carried out this by despatching a deputation consisting of three cardinals, S John and S Paul, S Pudenziana, and S Maria in Portico, to meet Frederic at S. Quirico, to endeavour to open negotiations with the Emperor, and to discover his intentions; also, if possible, to obtain his aid in capturing Arnold of Brescia out of the hands of the rebellious nobles of the Campagna. The embassy started on its errand, and Adrian waited quietly in Rome till he should hear the result

He must have been anxious indeed : for if an enemy, here was a far more formidable one than the excitable, injudicious Arnold, a warrior flushed with success, who was accustomed to dictate his own terms, backed up by all the power of Germany. What would be the conditions demanded if Rome became a beaten foe ? But Adrian continued to carry on his pontifical duties calmly and quietly, ready for whatever action he felt would be justified in upholding the high dignity of the Church It was in the meantime Frederic's intention to receive the imperial crown at the hands of the Pope; so he was, in a sense, coming in peace, and was prepared to treat, though he had no intention of giving up any right or dignity which he conceived that he possessed in his worldly title At the same time, as Adrian IV. had despatched his cardinals, Frederic had sent two envoys to treat with the Pope in the persons of the Archbishops of Cologne and of Ravenna, who were to ascertain whether the Pope was ready to receive their master in state and invest him with the imperial crown at S Peter's.

These two important embassies crossed each other without knowing it, and thus it came about that when Frederic's messengers to Rome arrived in the presence of Adrian IV., they were unable to tell him the result of his message to the Emperor. Before their arrival Adrian IV had gone to Civita Castellana[1] in case of another outbreak in the city, or so as to be in a fortified place under his own absolute power if the crisis ripened into difficulties with the Emperor. Here the archbishops came; the Pope took at once the firm, bold stand consistent with his character, and having made himself sure that no answer had been sent in return to his messages, absolutely refused to consider any of the proposals of the Emperor until he should have heard definitely the view Frederic was going to take about Arnold and the report of the cardinals he had sent; also he told the envoys that a preliminary to any negotiations must be a declaration from the Emperor that no hostility was intended.

We must now follow the fortunes of our northward journeying cardinals. They found Frederic Barbarossa strongly encamped with his powerful army at S Quirico in Tuscany, and were received, much to their relief, with every honour Like the Pope, however, Frederic declined to treat until he had heard of the reception his own ambassadors had met with at the hands of the Pontiff

[1] On the borders of the Campagna, about midway between Viterbo and Rome.

They, however, learnt one important thing, and that was that the Emperor considered Arnold of Brescia as an enemy to the imperial interests as well as to the papal authority, and in no way countenanced either his acts or those of the senate of Rome. This cleared the air considerably, for it showed that whatever Frederic's ultimate intentions might be, he at any rate regarded the Pope as supreme in Roman territory.

This encouraged the Cardinals to again urge that part of their instructions which related to Arnold, and as the Emperor was still much incensed by that demagogue's letter to him on his accession, which he regarded as impertinent and fanatical, they were able to play on his outraged feelings, and induced Frederic to promise to put his words into force and make Arnold a prisoner. With the power at his hand this was easy, as the nobles of the Campagna dared not resist the conqueror of Lombardy, Piedmont, and Tuscany; so despatching a force sufficient to overawe his protectors, Arnold fell a prey into his hands and was brought in chains to the camp.

Arnold had played his game boldly, but dangerously; he had disputed the power of the Pope and also had dared to dictate to the proudest monarch in Christendom, and had thereby brought the irresistible force of both potentates to unite against himself. He had staked all and lost, and in losing had destroyed his cause. Frederic handed him over to the Romans, and released the Campagnian nobles he had seized as hostages for his safe delivery.

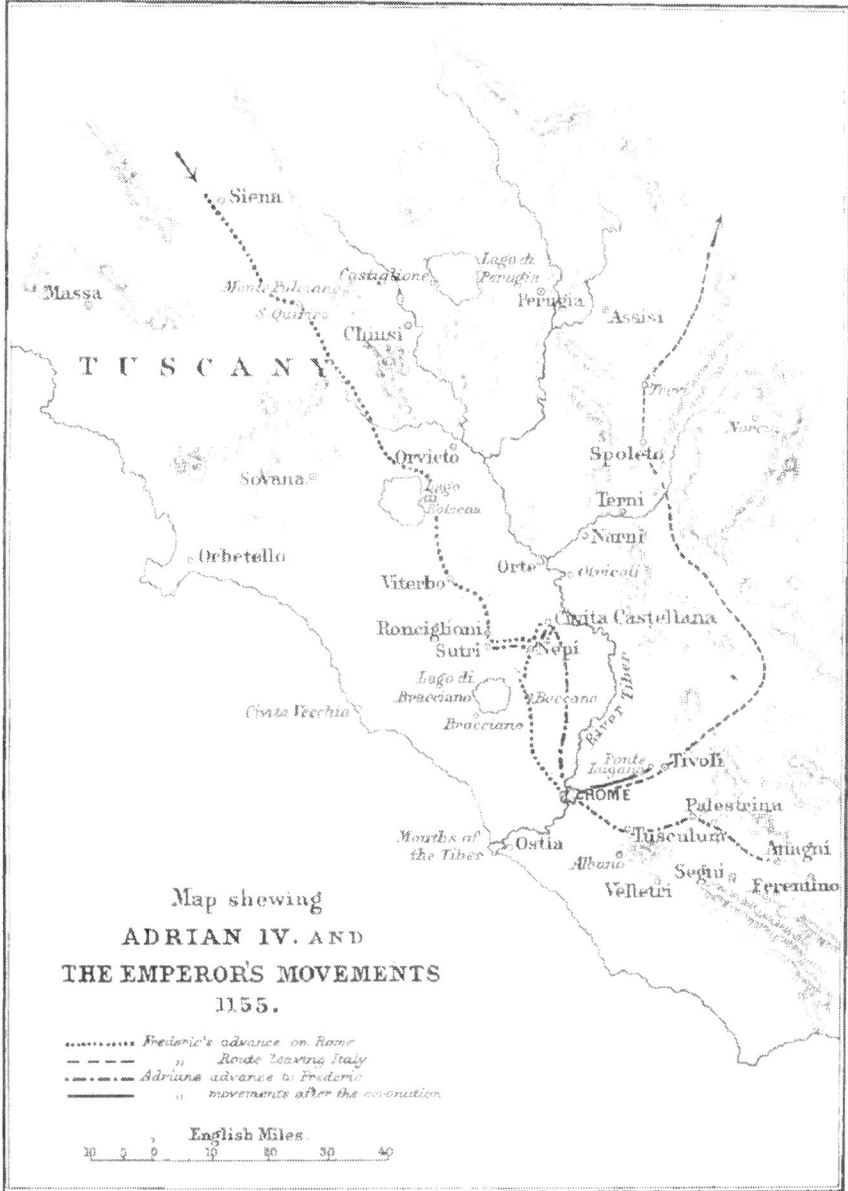

Map shewing

ADRIAN IV. AND
THE EMPEROR'S MOVEMENTS
1155.

.... *Frederic's advance on Rome*
— — — ,, *Route leaving Italy*
·—·—·— *Adrian's advance to Frederic*
━━━━━ ,, *movements after the coronation*

English Miles.

10   5   0   10   20   30   40

Arnold's thoughts must indeed have been bitter as he travelled with his escort to Rome,—the liberator in chains!

In the meantime Frederic had advanced to Viterbo, and so was now within a few miles of the Pope, who was still at Civita Castellana The two embassies in returning to their respective sovereigns met, and, holding a council together, determined to return to Frederic and endeavour to arrange terms of meeting between the two   Arnold of Brescia on arrival at Rome was imprisoned in the Castle of S. Angelo, in the custody of Cardinal Boso, whom Adrian had left in charge of his stronghold in Rome   The most important post of honour, he had chosen him as his most trusted adherent, and relied on him to keep the ever-rebellious senate in check, who were, even after their sharp lesson in Lent, again conspiring and watching for another opportunity of riot and revolution amongst the easily-inflamed citizens of Rome

We now come to a dark and awful episode in our history   The presence of Arnold as a prisoner was the greatest danger to peace which could be imagined. Most of the papal troops were in garrison in the fortified posts in the Campagna; some to the north; others in the south, on account of the advance of the armies of the King of Sicily, which I shall soon have to relate. Two dangers presented themselves to those left in charge of Adrian's interests The one, that of a successful revolt in favour of Arnold, in which case, what excuse might not Frederic make of it

P

to assume absolute power in Rome? With the great
ceremonials of coronation looming in the near future, a
fresh interdict of course was out of the question On the
other hand, if, as Frederic intended, Arnold was kept a
prisoner till the arrival of the Emperor, might he not
by his eloquence induce him to consider himself a
useful check on the power of the Pope, and so destroy
the firm basis of power and majesty which Adrian was
beginning to build? It must be remembered that those
left in this post of double danger could not know of
Frederic's animosity against Arnold; to them all was still
uncertain and the only way to ensure peace, and strike
fear into the hearts of the people, was the removal of
their leader The Church took the law into its own hands,
and, early one morning in June, the wretched man was led
out and secretly put to death There are various accounts
of this , but it seems generally agreed that he was fastened
to a cross and burnt alive , his ashes were flung into the
Tiber to prevent their being collected and made into a
national relic , the execution was carried out with haste for
fear of the people So ended the life of the fiery, obstinate
reformer

In judging the act of execution we must be careful not
to measure the sentiments of those days by the moral
standard of our own, and Arnold's death seems to have
been the only course left to those responsible to the Pope
for the order of the city On the other hand, we must
apply some moral standard to acts like this, and not allow

the consideration of difference in custom and thought to weigh against the sentiment of justice. Rarely, if ever, in history, is there an occasion when the execution of a man without trial can be excused And I regret to say that in describing the horrors of Arnold's death as related by Sismondi,[1] a Roman Catholic writer, whose history is in other respects admirable and impartial,[2] attempts to excuse the cruelties which were committed by saying that, however shocking it may seem to enlightened benevolence, yet from the Church point of view, viz., that the visible punishment of a crime should be commensurate with, and symbolize its moral enormity, the culprit received no more than he deserved. I do not attempt to minimize the crimes of Arnold of Brescia, but I cannot help mentioning this as illustrating the tendency of the Roman Church to regard all new theories as heretical, and to preserve that attitude towards improvement and progress which has lost the whole body of the Holy Catholic Church so much, lying as it does at the root, not only of our many unhappy divisions, but of much of the scepticism of the present day This sentiment strained to its logical conclusion may be used to justify all the horrors of the Inquisition, many of the so-called religious wars, and also

---

[1] Sismondi gives a dramatic account of the slow burning of Arnold fastened to a cross at the Porta del Popolo, which is not verified by early authors, and is characterized by Dean Milman as "pure fiction" (Milman, "Latin Christianity," vol iv , book viii., chap. vii, pp 412, 413, etc)

[2] R. Raby, "Life of Adrian IV ," p 41

to assume absolute power in Rome? With the great ceremonials of coronation looming in the near future, a fresh interdict of course was out of the question. On the other hand, if, as Frederic intended, Arnold was kept a prisoner till the arrival of the Emperor, might he not by his eloquence induce him to consider himself a useful check on the power of the Pope, and so destroy the firm basis of power and majesty which Adrian was beginning to build? It must be remembered that those left in this post of double danger could not know of Frederic's animosity against Arnold; to them all was still uncertain, and the only way to ensure peace, and strike fear into the hearts of the people, was the removal of their leader. The Church took the law into its own hands, and, early one morning in June, the wretched man was led out and secretly put to death. There are various accounts of this, but it seems generally agreed that he was fastened to a cross and burnt alive; his ashes were flung into the Tiber to prevent their being collected and made into a national relic; the execution was carried out with haste for fear of the people. So ended the life of the fiery, obstinate reformer.

In judging the act of execution we must be careful not to measure the sentiments of those days by the moral standard of our own, and Arnold's death seems to have been the only course left to those responsible to the Pope for the order of the city. On the other hand, we must apply some moral standard to acts like this, and not allow

the consideration of difference in custom and thought to
weigh against the sentiment of justice. Rarely, if ever, in
history, is there an occasion when the execution of a man
without trial can be excused   And I regret to say that in
describing the horrors of Arnold's death as related by
Sismondi,[1] a Roman Catholic writer, whose history is in
other respects admirable and impartial,[2] attempts to excuse
the cruelties which were committed by saying that, however shocking it may seem to enlightened benevolence,
yet from the Church point of view, viz., that the visible
punishment of a crime should be commensurate with,
and symbolize its moral enormity, the culprit received
no more than he deserved.   I do not attempt to minimize
the crimes of Arnold of Brescia, but I cannot help mentioning this as illustrating the tendency of the Roman Church
to regard all new theories as heretical, and to preserve
that attitude towards improvement and progress which
has lost the whole body of the Holy Catholic Church so
much, lying as it does at the root, not only of our many
unhappy divisions, but of much of the scepticism of the
present day. This sentiment strained to its logical conclusion may be used to justify all the horrors of the
Inquisition, many of the so-called religious wars, and also

[1] Sismondi gives a dramatic account of the slow burning of Arnold
fastened to a cross at the Porta del Popolo, which is not verified by early
authors, and is characterized by Dean Milman as "pure fiction" (Milman,
"Latin Christianity," vol iv , book viii., chap vii , pp 412, 413, etc)
[2] R. Raby, "Life of Adrian IV ," p 41.

dream of bestowing the imperial crown on an emperor
who came from Swabia, and was not Roman by birth or
nationality

After this preamble,[1] in itself superbly injudicious and
tactless, they proceeded to formulate their demands, in which
they commanded him to respect all their ancient institutions
and laws, to protect them against neighbouring powers, to
take their part in disputes with the Pope, and to pay a sum
of 5,000 pounds of silver as an indemnity

They wound up by demanding a solemn oath from
Frederic to maintain the republic, if necessary, with the help
of the sword, and to seal this agreement as a perpetual
treaty   The great Barbarossa seems to have contained his
rage at first, even amid the angry mutterings of his knights
and suite, and, after a pause, he began a calm, dignified
reply.   He quietly corrected their view of the history of
Rome by relating at equal length the case of Charlemagne
and the transfer of the imperial power to him and his suc-
cessors   Then, waiting to let his words sink in, he loosed
his tongue, and, amid thunders of applause from his nobles,
roared out at the frightened envoys, while pointing to the
circle behind him.   " Here are my Teutonic nobles, my
banded chivalry, your only laws are those I choose to
enact, your only liberty is allegiance to me, your sovereign "[2]

[1] Gunther, iii, p 450, et seq
[2] For the text of this address, and the Emperor's reply, see Gibbon's
" Decline and Fall of the Roman Empire,' edition of 1855, in eight vols,
with notes by Milman and Guizot, vol viii, cap lxix, pp 206, 207, 209

This was the haughty and humiliating reply to the forwardness of the Roman senate The deputation withdrew amid the jeers and taunts of the Germans, and wended their crestfallen way back to Rome, with the news that these rough soldiers, who called themselves nobles, were styled by Frederic the perpetual senate of Rome ! Now came the turn of the ambassadors of the Pope who returned with Frederic's own envoys. They had a favourable interview with the Emperor, and were able to take back to Adrian the Emperor's solemn promise that he had no hostile intentions whatever against the Pope, that he was ready to pay all honour to the Holy Church and the see of Rome, and asked if Adrian would publicly and with all solemnity crown him in S Peter's

Adrian was cautious; and just as in Norway he laid down his conditions before granting the favour asked, so now did he determine to extract a solemn oath from the Emperor first,[1] and to obtain all the guarantees that were possible for keeping him to his word. He sent word to Frederic, who was encamped at Sutri, that if he swore on the gospels and on the cross before the papal ambassadors that he would protect the Pope and all his cardinals against aggression, and would uphold the dignity of the papal office, nor usurp any of its functions, he would ride out to meet him, and would not only crown him as he wished, but would accompany him in state into Rome. Adrian's

---

[1] Muratori, vol vii, p 135.

demands were complied with [1] In solemn state, bare-
headed, and with uplifted sword, the Emperor solemnly
gave his oath to the cardinals and kissed the sacred
volume handed to him, then, on his knees, surrounded by
his court, he reverently saluted the cross also

With joy the cardinals departed, and Adrian promised
to ride out and meet the Emperor   Thus had he obtained
the interview he required without any loss of the dignity
which he considered due to his high office   He was well
aware, however, that the crisis was only approaching, it was
not sufficient that the Emperor should merely declare his
allegiance to the Church, backed though the declaration
might be by any number of solemn oaths, it was necessary
that in his own person, in the presence of his own people,
the mighty conqueror should do homage before the Vicar
of Christ for his kingdom

This claim to such homage may seem mere haughti-
ness on the part of the Church, the homage itself a
degradation to the Emperor ; but it must be remembered
that the Pope represented literally to the minds of all
devout Christians our Blessed Lord Himself, and, however great the earthly potentate, he lost none of his dignity
in the eyes of the faithful by doing homage to the Holy
Father, as he was thereby regarded as actually prostrating
himself at the feet of the Saviour's own person

How Adrian IV gained this most important point

[1] 8th June, 1155

Lightning Source UK Ltd.
Milton Keynes UK
UKHW022335060223
416579UK00001B/18

9 781354 399927